Praise for *Sing Past Winter*...

"Ms. Jacoby Lopez's accomplished artwork graces the bone-deep struggle for consciousness expressed in her evocative—often erotic—poetry. *Sing Past Winter* warmed my heart into spring and summer. It is an extraordinary wedding of body and soul."
—DARYL SHARP
Publisher, Inner City Books, Toronto, Canada

"We need a language to negotiate our passions, losses, and loves. Poetry is that language, and Margaret Jacoby Lopez not only is fluent but has been to the depths."
—ALAN JONES
Dean, Grace Cathedral, San Francisco, author of *Living the Truth* and *Seasons of Grace*

""*Sing Past Winter*...comes to me like an echo in a high mountain valley that signals the presence of another pilgrim at the same time that it resonates in the vast silence of my own solitude. It both comforts me and reminds me that the soul's journey is a lonely one, and not for the faint of heart ..."
—SAM KEEN
Author of *Fire in the Belly* and *Learning to Fly*

"Margaret Jacoby Lopez's poetry and paintings in *Sing Past Winter* are remarkable forms of a deep sacramental/mystical sensibility. She has, through her own suffering, plumbed a depth of consciousness that is close to the numinous."
—EUGENE MONICK
Priest, Jungian analyst, author of *Phallos*

"[This book] runs the gamut from doubt to deep belief and portrays the continuous struggle, the going back and forth from the divine to the human. Self-searching, philosophical, spiritual (and unabashedly so) . . . this is brave poetry."
—DAVID DODD LEE
Poet and author of *Arrow Pointing North* and *Downsides of Fish Culture*

"With words and images of dark beauty, the author gives our imaginations play and challenge. She doesn't deny death; with its generative force she empowers life. Her work is a testament to and poetic extension of Ernest Becker's *Denial of Death*. We sing together."
—NEIL ELGEE
Executive director, Ernest Becker Foundation

"This treasure is so beautiful it will be read long after we are all gone."
—CHAKRAPANI ULLAL, Vedic astrologer

Sing Past Winter is an extraordinary banquet for the senses of the soul. The artwork is a feast for the eyes. The poetry longs to be spoken aloud. This is a rich treat that must be enjoyed as a slow meal, a meal that will last for years."
—JUSTINE AND MICHAEL TOMS
New Dimensions World Broadcasting Network
Authors of *True Work . . . Doing What You Love and Loving What You Do*

"Margaret Jacoby Lopez has created a portal through which spirit may flow into our lives. As we contemplate these majestic images and words, we touch the transcendent and are transformed."
—BARBARA MONTGOMERY DOSSEY
Author of *Florence Nightingale, Rituals of Healing,* and *Holistic Nursing*

Sing Past Winter is more like a healing than a book. This magnificent contribution requires meditation, concentration, and great thoughtfulness—and it repays handsomely. Like all great art and wisdom, this is a distillation of elegance, simplicity, and beauty."
—LARRY DOSSEY
Author of *Healing beyond the Body, Reinventing Medicine,* and *Healing Words*

"This extraordinary work brings one woman's journey to an archetypal level that opens the heart and mind of anyone who encounters the words and images. What a brave, true, and beautiful endeavor."
—ROSHI JOAN JIKO HALIFAX
Head teacher, Upaya Zen Center Santa Fe, author of *Shaman* and *The Fruitful Darkness*

"Here is a guide through the oldest human song of birth, death, and resurrection. Margaret is a cross-disciplinary artist whose original voice combines collage with innovative painting, print, and poetic text. She has through her unusual journey of creation discovered the universal voice of love. She holds a fresh vision of genius for the mysterious human evolution from within."
—SILYA KIESE
Interdisciplinary artist, writer, and educator, New York

Sing Past Winter is a journey of love, recognition, death, and restoration told with truth, beauty, elegance, and wisdom. The imagery washes over you, leaving you feeling cleansed, fresh, awakened."
—RHEA GOODMAN
Host, KSFR Radio, Santa Fe

Sing Past Winter is a testament to the human struggle to acknowledge our wounds and despair, and to reach further to affirm faith, hope, and love. Margaret Jacoby Lopez has offered us a mirror to reflect our own transformation."
—LINDA SCHIERSE LEONARD
Author of *The Wounded Woman* and *The Call to Create*

SING PAST WINTER

Sing Past Winter

A MODERN PSALTER

Margaret Jacoby Lopez

BLUE
FIRE
BOOKS

Santa Fe, New Mexico

Published by Blue Fire Books
            21 Hawthorne Circle
            Santa Fe, NM 87506

Editor: Ellen Kleiner
Book design and typography: Janice St. Marie
Cover design: Swell Design, Inc.
Paintings: M. Jacoby Lopez

Printed in the United States of America on acid-free recycled paper

Lopez, Margaret Jacoby.
      Sing past winter : a modern psalter / Margaret
      Jacoby Lopez. -- Santa Fe, N.M. : Blue Fire Books, 2003.

        p. ; cm.
        ISBN 0-9729834-1-4

        1. Spiritual healing. 2. Mind and body. 3. Nature,
      Healing power of. 4. Women artists--Biography.
      5. Women poets--Biography. 6. Psalters. I. Title.

BF161 .L67 2003   2003104539

150--dc21   0309

10 9 8 7 6 5 4 3 2 1

FOR TOM

IN GRATITUDE . . .

To Barbara Witt, who designed the prototype for this book and who took most of the photographs for the paintings, which I rendered in acrylic, charcoal, ash, and collage

David Dodd Lee, from whom I learned so much about verse and finding my own voice

Duncan, Dianne, and Tim, for being the most excellent models

Sue, for the ritual that created the ash sealing the artwork

Pat Moffitt Cook, for introducing me to the power of cross-cultural sound, which assisted my healing

Patricia, Darla, Sylvia, Janet, Don, and Alice Jean, who listened to, lived, and loved the whole story

Jack Blackburn for being my spiritual guide and helping me access my creativity in a new way

Gail Larsen, who inspired me to bring this book to the world

And to Ellen, for her skillful editing and for overseeing the production; Janice, for her creative concept for the interior of the book; and Linda, Robin, and Dana, for designing the cover.

CONTENTS

Dusk wraps the valley floor.
The owl's flight beats back night, and then it happens.
It is as if darkness rose from the meadow
and descended from the sky to meet just above
the trees. At that moment all is still ... Listen.

FOREWORD

Within these pages are the struggles of a soul becoming free. This is not the journey of a timid soul. I have had the good fortune to accompany Margaret Jacoby Lopez as she undertook this heartfelt path and journeyed into terra incognita with her soul as her guide. Her experience has been filled with wonderment and dismay … for inside, the landscapes are so totally different. This soul is proclaiming the experiences of the body are not the end point but a pathway to higher truth. Nature, stillness, and silence become the most reliable companions.

The illustrations, true to the feelings of the poems, take us deeply within the experience of the embodied soul. Together they help us penetrate the dark corners of the psyche.

Travel with Margaret as a pilgrim and try on the mantle of courage and determination evoked from these challenging words and images. You will start to feel your own power as your truth is revealed.

JACK BLACKBURN

THORNS AND MEMORIES

Is it the rip in my heart that accepts my longing
and grants me hope to stretch further than my reach,
or is it creation's hand stretching the hymen of God's nature
for me to claim my divinity's weakness?
A confession of silent thoughts that shocks my desire
to touch the place where eruptions start to confound my love.

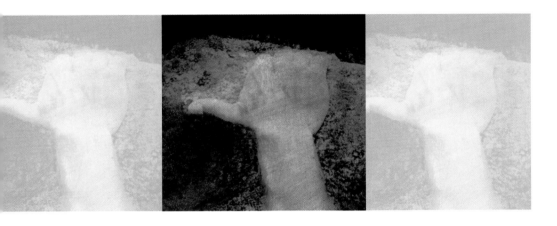

Is it my fault that maturity has sentenced me to decay
leaving me youth's shyness and excusing the ultimate fear
to go further and push against the weakness of God?
Is it my fault that grown-up tears stain my face
giving away the coming attraction
to be revealed when my body of beliefs is rescued by heartbreak
and creation's thorn is dug out of my head for all to see—

a blood-soaked brow reminding me to have or have not
as much or as little as desired?
Each thorn like nettles stings my memory
of bones, dislocation, forgetting,
brightens passion's passing of time eternal.
Eternity has no hand to tell it by;
God's nature is to remember
and God's weakness is to keep it going,
lusting after every creature
whose thought and experience become the gift.

Are thoughts and experiences alone worth dying for?
Is the kiss of betrayal an experience worth dying for?
If it is, what am I missing?
If it isn't, then what is this tiny cross in my hand—
gift of my broken heart?

What is this love penetrating me?
the first tiny rip I've been dying for—
an opening into myself
stretched by another to taste purpose pungent with blood,
accepting each plucked thorn;
violin breaking my heart.
Beethoven's pain, an aching for joy,
arouses this ecstatic little light of mine
with all its goodness and courage—
sweetest belief pure and simple.
God is in the twenty-third psalm
waiting in the shadow of the valley
and my death is my weakness.
And it is in this weakness my hope stretches,
it is in this weakness my belief is shocked,
it is the impossible released in surrender to insanity
for my mind is pierced by improbable freedom,
my heart set up to be broken.

Let my divinity claim my fears
for I am bound in weakness since birth.

What species am I at this border crossing?
Am I born both animal and human,
moving on my belly through Eden
tempting you to share your desires with me
in that secret place mortals crave?
Mortal love bursts past the fears
that block the body's feelings,
allowing instinct to live in the moment—
alert, afraid, shy to divinity's purpose—
telling the truth about love.

I cannot love you until I love myself.
I cannot know you until I know myself.

Animal, alien, mortal,
God moving amongst us,
deeper than the self,
each moment building the forgotten next.
No one will remember their beliefs.
Beliefs can't set us free.

It is weakness that sets us free,
weakness that breaks the heart.

You have broken mine and in giving you the pieces
I accept your vulnerability as a thorn,
for you didn't ask for my heart, you prayed for it,
you prayed to be open to receive
and I prayed for your heart, broken,
to see clearly a vision, a destiny,
a lively offering to each other
where we are covered by love's mantle,
protecting us, revealing us no longer separate
but one heart—
a witness to each other's pain,
for pain revealed is pain relieved.

You are pain. I am not.
I am pain. You are not.
You are Christ. I am not.
I am Christ. You are not,
and when I am not
I lose my mind,
and when I lose my mind
I go looking for yours.

I need your heart to recognize who I am.

For what is pain without recognition?
What is pleasure without recognition?
What is joy without recognition?
Is joy recognition of pain made holy?
Joy is holy pleasure recognized as fragile,
conjugally joined for a moment,
shaking out sorrow
permeating the body with sweat,
the mind with sound,
the spirit shot with light.

We are the toast of this generation—
Two cups raised as one,
sorrow mingled with myrrh,
tiny drops of blood,
red circles staining the table.

A fused union hears the heartbeat.
Sighing, sinking, echoing
drifting out into the other
opening the eyelids to behold—
a pair of eyes closed
the mouth open
as if the last breath had been breathed
the last kiss tasted,
the last throb, the last pulse
the last ache subsiding in our bodies
two cups drained, and turned upside down
on the stained table,
our voices whisper one last time,
Take me as I am.

the

crescent

moon

Holy moment of recognition.
It is a relief knowing what you are thinking.
The self afraid of the self,
tempting happiness.

The serpent spoke to me
and told me I was evil,
and I believed I was
until I exchanged evil for weakness
and opened myself to life.

I carry the imprint of Lionheart, thorn of truth.

How far can I break, how far can I see inside myself?
Should I wait by the side of my bed
expecting some revelation
like the touch of an angelic being laying me down
or the shadow of an owl passing the window?
What if nothing happens?
What if the light doesn't fade
and darkness doesn't close in?
What if nothing happens?
I'm waiting for you to show me what I'm missing.
I'm no longer young; tears grant me grace.
I am going to say this one more time and see how it sounds:
"I am shy to my divinity."
This is not an idea.

It is a memory of ripping fabric
to reach the spot where attraction is whole.

CROWN

The fool says in the heart there is no God.
Inside of this idea is a wordless encounter with death.
Outside of this idea is memory sticking life to death,
an oxygenated idea holding the gravity of beliefs for one more day.

How many days does it take to say good-bye to an idea?
How many years to let memory drift?

On the third day, I watched the stone roll away
and the idea became a memory.
The spirit left me changed forever.

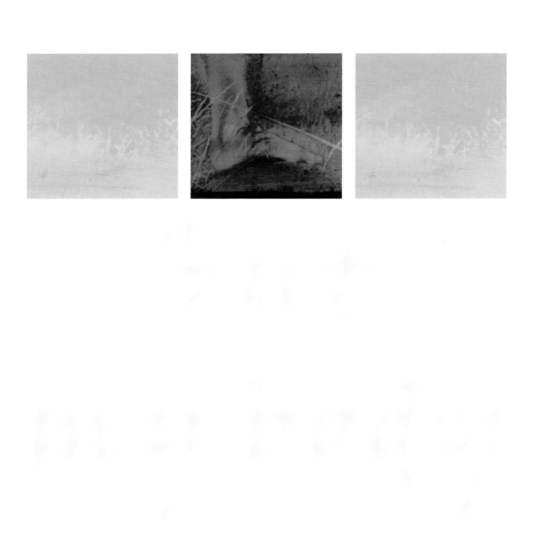

Christ rose in the heart, Buddha in the mind,
crowning nothing above and nothing below,
destroying me and pinning my heart to the fool
who wears the rose-red crown,
silver moon, stars stuck to the points,
pricking my temples with meaning and sweat,
dye stains running red down my face,
a ring of roses, crown of thorns or a hero's wreath
crush this brainless cavity of ideas with love,
empty architecture, obsolete skullcap,
mind gripped in the vice of light
freeing my heart to beat further
than desire to be neatly folded,
convention leaving nothing of this body to be admired
save poetry drawn hundreds of times,
squinting at the written word, smiling at the spoken.

Unspoken presence becomes the touch of kindness
and kindness is no fool.
Only a fool would be crowned with thorns.
You are my fool, I am yours,
you are my must fermenting self.
You crown me with laurel, I crown you with thorns—
hard pricks stabbing, ejaculating imagination,
to release God's weakness
where creativity seeks to be realized,
not where power is at the circumference
but where weakness pulses the center—
                    fear and love
satisfying our appetites for pleasure and lust,
God's search for the harvest of souls
watches them ripen in bodies revealed.

Grim reaper, come get me.
I've been ripened since three in my tiny bed
feeling pleasure, not pain at my desire
finding the vulnerable place in God is my place.
The rip in my heart
is the way into the pleasure of God.

Nothing, everything, seen, unseen,
aromatic, salty taste senses beneath my presence
demanding the key to the trapdoor of nothing
climbing down the ladder of nothing
to the hall of mirrors, life's maze of distortions—
deformity to giggle at, horrified it might be me
relieved it isn't, striking the gorgeous pose,
hiding out to kiss and exchange secrets
leaving behind one set of bad habits for another,
all dispensable.

Where will you be when I'm nothing?
You will be everything that's left.

Prepare ye the bunker of the Lord.

The host is upon us.

Our bones are hot, melting our marrow.

There is nothing left to risk.

We are finished in this place.

Night burns and brands me a new creature.

Dying means living through the pain of birth

and I was the only one who could tell what it was like.

NATIVITY

sizzle   flash   pop
Primal interference envelops light.
Darkness envelops silence,
silence holds its breath.

It couldn't be mine. I didn't want a doll.
Thankless, I held my breath—
one   two   three
Breathe or I'll smash your head.
I'll rip off your arms. Your legs, I'll break.
Breathe, human, see how it feels.
Lie under the tree, genderless doll, and mock me, naked.

We were barely alive at our nativity.
We saw shyness in each other's eyes
and held our breath to block our feelings
from the idea that it might be mine or yours.
Shy nativity, our divinity . . .
love came down and touched us in an improbable way;
it was a love story, imperfect and dangerous.

The path from the manger was narrow
winding out of lifetimes
farther than I could see into lifetimes.
This was not a belief or an idea.
It was animal nature, pantheistic,
holding us in the crib side by side,
bough rocking darkness into light,
together, open to each other's moment of inspiration—
            bare birth
sticky hands revealed an instinct to wet-nurse our love
and keep us on earth long enough to receive our gifts
pain   hope   joy
holy gifts for holy children—

fragile nativity fell for love,

new love is our love

and love is new to birth, woven in and out of touch,

creative tension pushing us from our crib

into a cat's cradle for play

licking, biting, trying out an idea or two—

three cheers for God's fool

for only in God's weakest moment

could we have been born.

Birth committed to memory cannot be undone.
Love can chance encounter
find ideas to tease eternity's intention to remember
exchange a thorn for love to draw out truth,
joy greater than our desiring.

SACRIFICE

Perfect, the cat, watching row upon row of brethren

vast seas of body prayers,

feline stretch, head to the ground, ass in the air,

rows of asses reflected in amber eyes,

vulnerability rolled back. Perfect stretched

farther than Abraham could reach,

pressing his gorgeous body to the blood-stained rock

witness to the idea of a father's sacrifice.

Only a fool would kill his son;

only a fool loses love.

it

was

close

Perfectly stretched, my dust pressed to yours

I saw the blade raised in air.
Eros, kill me with mercy
kill all of me; leave only my tongue
for in my tongue all desires are satisfied.
I sing and curse my maker.
I commit myself to you and savor your lips
open to me (only the tiniest crack).

Touch my tongue, fleshly muscle,
the taste of weakness,
God in my mouth
body to bread, blood to wine;
divine fool, your sacrifice is over.

The Sufi master of the world stood before me and tied my tongue.

If I imagined him, then he imagined me

to be his vision as he was mine

arousing wordless intercourse

creating us out of nothing—

tongues to speak of something.

What do I do with love? Let it go? Leave it, or look?
The voice from our hearts beat in my inner ear:

"Leave the stones where they are under your feet.

Leave the sun where it is in the heavens.

Leaving is nothing for a vision,

for a body it is sacrifice of all beliefs.

Go deeper than all beliefs,

for love in this body is belief in consequences.

Go deeper than this.

Consequences are stones—

keep them under your feet, where they can't harm you.

This love is more than being struck with a stone,

this love is incarnation of infinite possibilities."

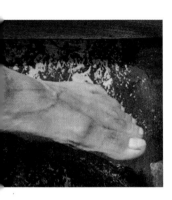 

Perfect watched the sea of adoring bodies kneel;
he could not be stoned
during a ritual of collective prayer.

True seekers of God were welcome at his rock.
Bodies bowed; without moving an inch or a whisker
the Sufi master of the world left me shoeless
feeling stones that could kill me under my feet, bruised.
Lovers choose sacrifice—
pain calls us out of the world
and into an infancy that cries for the face of love
not words of holy wisdom but a face to refract our light,
a face of courage, divinity,
not hidden in a ritual fog of beauty
refusing to look at individual truth.

Stone me or stone me not,
my body recognizes the fragrance of love
imperfect perfect improbable love.

IMAGINE ME

Divinity claims nothing but refrain,
mortals claim everything to death.

Joining is our weakness;
separation, transcendence.

The age-old story repeats
its power to return to life again,
delivered of uncertainty
with the uncommon ash of devotion
scattered on air,
materialized divinity everywhere.

The stars become your eyes,
the clouds your disguise.
If you can, imagine you, imagine me
when we again are joined in infancy.

DIVINITY

Divinity's weakness is the taste that mortals bring.
Bodies: an offering
returned for God's consuming gift. Pain
to satisfy the sacrifice again

and hope my soul finally sees
one spirit, through my body's victory
recognized the moment I start
to need each shadow of my heart

for you and I, once silent in our night
brought all the uncreated sounds to light
for joy I know it. See it be—
it is our moment of divinity.

DEVOTION

The world's face is my face
leaves turn as does my cheek

my failure to see, listen, speak

lost or found, history crumbles
Corinthian temples
into sands, quiet praise

beggars' bowls fill with silence
tarnished with the ring of devotion.

Hush! simple desire
to be creator and created,
impressing who, me or you?

Desire turns one universe
into another, willing the spirit to repeat,

Love if named is nothing.

Fight the meaning: mind of one is seed of the other,
heart of one is love of the other cast in front of us.

Which century's bones are the subject?
Whose story is told?

Christ's, Mohammed's, Buddha's

the wealth scattered on every shore
picked over by thousands

found by few, treasured,
secret perfection

singular devotion.

On white shore I take up the watch,
head bowed, I search grains and grains and grains
endless hours . . .

My eyes move faster than my feet
broken day is night

erasing my prints but not your face
drawn from my memory

dilemma of impermanence
your love draws me closer
than my body's desire to love captivity.

Your flesh now thin as freedom's veil
is thinner than stretched skin

full to bursting with life
from oceans away delivering me a rare find—

the black shell.

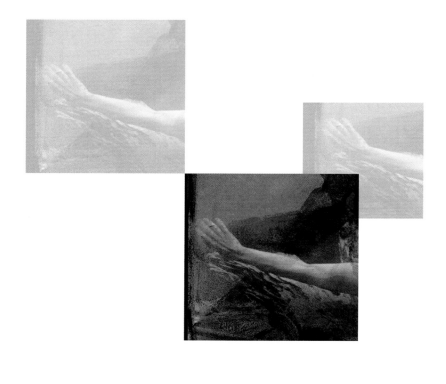

Sunrise comes again and blinds our expectancy
plainer though we may be

beyond youth's impulse to procreate
is devotion's desire to re-create.

Are we born of each other's soul?

Is life God's love pulsing through our bodies?

Our hunger, sands and shells satisfy,
as smells and tastes change perfume to balm.

Your love for me is like a grain of sand doubled,
pressed one into the other with desire
multiplied
like white talc
stuck to my skin,
proof inexhaustible that everything from dusk
to dawn is mine,

even season's change.

Desert sands blow bodies red
orchards stain us green.

your
weight

Trees leaf and flower their purpose with abundance.

Hunger, my purpose, wills a branch to break

dropping fruit inside me.

You are now in me. I ate your seed.

I am satisfied but you are never.

And when you want another more than me

I germinate and grow and present

you with more than you have given.

Better to learn our lessons from despair and love affairs
than from a book of hours

to look at altars
spread and glimpse the mystery

to understand the faith that made
the food, the drink, the cloth, the light;

the prayer bowl begs, it's empty still . . .
silence, the treasure held

within my hands, what's lost is found.
The black shell, devotion is.

REFRAIN

Breath is my impulse
awe is my prayer
devotion my food
for in me you're there.

Love is the subject; a faith unfolds
of quiet devotion pressed into gold
thin veil of ages my soul secrets me
flowers plucked from a story of old century.

The earth is my center, dark at the core;
my heart broken open, my spirit's eye saw
a piece of the map sketched deep in the sands
of silent devotion sifting time through my hands.

We are earth's coals blackened and bright
our dust drops beneath, surrounding us white
sparks under our words, embers above,
fire set by our glow, burn us with love.

Our ashes will mix on this earth we call home
but until we burn out, don't leave us alone.
You're invited to kindle, I'll tend you till done
two coals together burn brighter than one.

You move me around with the air of your breath
you toss me and catch me and prepare me for death
you twist me and turn me and tease me and still
you leave me alone and grant me my will.

The veil thin
is freedom and in freedom we'll be
carried by our senses
to another century.

A NEW THING

Rooted nature clings to nothing
to be a new thing.

Flowerless trees stretch sideways to a world
where leaves compose frail matter
weathered by hours, the countdown continues
to mark creation's return.

My body is nature re-created in a new image
open to God's heart, in my spirit
a fresh face of love.

beside

me

My boneless ashes wash up on an eroding shore.

Nameless wave that carried them no more,

its impulse started oceans ago

as did my desire to land me a new thing . . .

We are in time; it is a good thing.
For love to grow we must be depleted
and say good-bye to all affairs
that hold us from our nature
and like the leaf budded full, fall, fade
be carried on the wind.

pressing

Eternity begins when we begin
to move aside, draw the inscription.

Who makes the finest mark in copperplate?
Let me, my life this fine thing make.
Let it be I who dies and lives within this authorship
for I am drawn on every street and wall.
Eternity appears before I trip and fall
or cast my eyes away, denying death.

Do I pretend that honest day
be wiser when from sleep I wake?

My dreams are nothing more
than desire filled to pick your pockets full

of wealth—for this I drop
my body's composition and accept

creation feeds
the one who needs it most.

Who chooses a broken heart
is satisfied with madness and lament,
for sadness calls us all by name
and so does grief.

Creation calls me lucky and so do you
when meadows flower without my point of view.

The sons and daughters are the lucky ones
who lose control of self, live the contradiction
of homeless birth. Their spirit lies with kings
and claims the enterprise for richer, poorer fame.
We're all Job's kin—no doubt we're called the same.

The one spirit, silent, beats in every breast its name.

For when I wake, you sleep forgetting me.
Eternity, I claim my time to be the potter's clay,
a natural state of ecstasy.

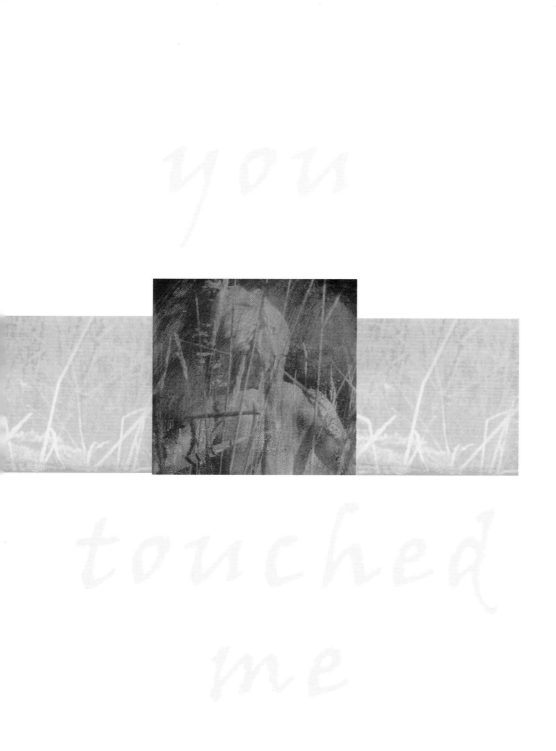

you

touched

me

Death's hands threw me upon the wheel of time
and gave it back in form unique—
God's satisfaction for my madness and my grief.

I claim creation's mine, for I need it most
and substitute my weakness for your voice.

Light cracks the father's darkest thought.
A new myth is given,
to build our stories from the tomb,
the day the child is born again.

My stained hand—
prints in the cave—
my dream enough for any service.

When I withhold my love
I exile spirit from my heart
that beats its nature into mind,
instinct into spirit,
fills the face of love
as Joseph filled his brother's sack
desiring to know the love that exiled him.

I'm purified by the sap of primal life.
Amber glows upon my hand
when I am born again.
If I receive the principle of love,
will you receive the gift of me?
Receive each other's spirit
the trinity of mind, impulse
and nature upon the heart.
One soul, one face, a new thing is.

VOICE OF THE SOUL

First Voice

Full voice of the soul
echo me, *bird, bee, running brook*
wash a rock a thousand times
shape singing stones, carry the celebration
one note to another, uncovering creation.

Full voice of the soul, ageless bright and beautiful
call out my vanity, my satisfaction.
In vain I search the mystery

and carry the consequence of a sound
desiring one cell to sound it back—
the one who fell with me in deep song
spirited through hope;
bring me my ashes for my trouble.

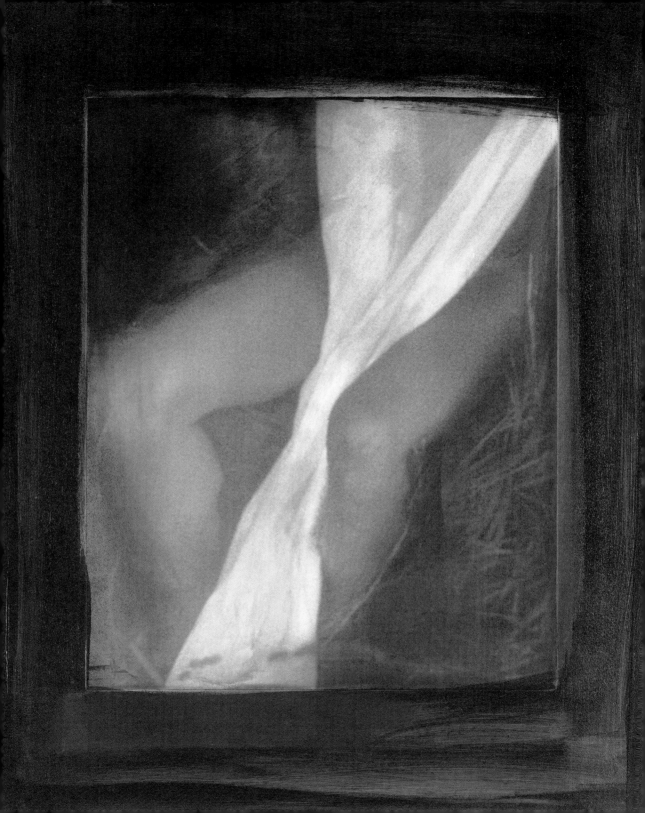

Second Voice

Full voice of the soul
lose me on the bridge over now
and find me when my time is due
for I am the consequence of two worlds joined,
stretched to the vanishing point beyond myself.

My voice, a hum inside my head,
is a lament growing my feelings
beyond bereavement, beyond friendship's privilege
pressed between the pages of history.
Timeless perfection sticks desire and happiness
with the waft of the soul's voice.

Silent conversation between I and thou, between me and thee
capturing Francis from Assisi,
John the beginning, Bach the bridge.
Universal voice higher and deeper than any dogma
Israel's hope born over and over
removes the speck in my eye, which waters
clearing the bias and delivering me of the prize—
alive and alive again.

Third Voice

Full voice of the soul
lay me down in the running brook of promise
wash my reward with wisdom.

Fresh splash, repeat each note
denoting a change, clear.
Spontaneous sound inward,
outward coming to terms with youth's swirling opus
leaving the mysterious conjunction
of past and future to measure time.

Fading light of beauty
hold and release my leaves on rafting riplets.
Move time's stones from the heart
of the running brook.

Quiet song, forget me not.

Fourth Voice

Full voice of the soul
surprise me in silence, wake the day.
Hand of dawn, shake this cold mortal with another
preserving sublime nature in our earthly innocence.

Clumsy brilliance waves at God with our bodies.
Unknown scent tickles our nostrils
eyes rubbed out of forgetfulness
ears pricked to catch only the faintest sound of closing day.

Full voice of the soul
crack the natural world with an unforgiving force
sound the soul's thunder, dangerous and beautiful—
this day's voice gone forever.

EXILE

Lord, surrender to me.
Name the prophetic bird that sings past winter.
Name the plant that bears spring.
Name the battle lost.
Which calf was killed?
Beat on the drum.
Drop your sickle, angel, and surrender.
Don't give your name, give another
and if it's mine and my body wins
I die in exile and you are
crowned on your own erection.

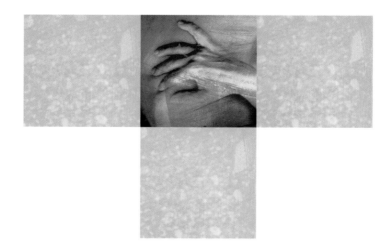

I shape shift—*el toro*—I die; die
and you inherit the ring.
Forty days is all you get to die; die
to be one with me in exile.
So, sweet God, hand me Christ.

Let me be the one; feel me more fully,
Let the sweat be mine—lingering fragrance
my body, be yours.
Let me enter in, my senses electrified.

It was then I entered through a human doorway
pulled past my body's breath.
Flutes played.
My nature echoed back
beyond my brain cells—detaching knowing.
I was not in me.
I was in the sound breaking over my sight—
    an opened vision.

My shadow anointed the light
with my nakedness furnished.
My childhood's quiver, red bow my passion,
rain tree honey enough for comfort,
my hands cupped full of memories—
Who am I?

First love is never lost;
it is reclaimed in exile.
Don't think destiny claims you,
think exile.
For exile is freedom.
Exile is nourishment of spirit.
Exile is the face of love.

The valley of my exile is full
of tall grasses
higher than my forehead.
I can see the sky
and two trees at the top of the hill—
one a pine, one a fir.

I did my best not to yield before the crescent moon
but my body had gone too far.
The hawk showed me his nest.
It was close to where we slept.
I felt your weight beside me pressing wildflowers;
you touched me awake.
When did you leave?

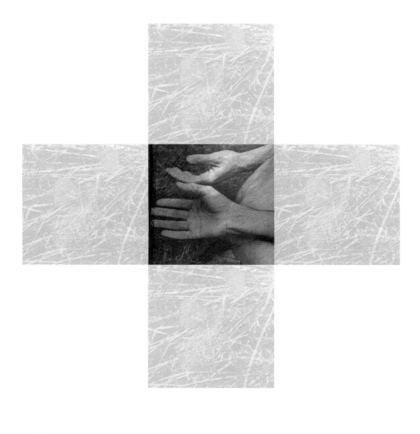

I am still here trying to remember what happened.
Did you bring me here to shed my old skin,
to lay the foundation for my departure
and to build an altar of ash and yew?

ARTIST'S NOTES

When a muse-filled poet surrenders to nature's mystery, divinity is revealed in human form—as male/female, reflecting the androgeny of spirit—and beheld as a key for unlocking the soul's voice. Other keys are in the landscape itself, their power deriving from centuries of collected memory that has penetrated them. Infused with universal and personal meaning, these symbols of divine encounter connect us with cultures and times beyond our own. Suddenly a union of two worlds is possible. External and internal are one. Ideas and images conspire with inspiration and memory. The improbable is anticipated, and when it occurs spirit radiates joy, giving each symbol fresh meaning and the capacity to penetrate more deeply.

Throughout this book, tiny symbols are acknowledged, such as the hawk's feather, the heart-shaped rock in the river, the black shell in the sand, the drum, the butterfly, the thistle, the antler, the bird's nest, fire, shadows on the tall grasses, three birds in a tree, ash, our human bodies. All have meaning. The lexicon that follows presents definitions distilled from myth of select terms and images appearing in these pages. May they invite further discovery.

ASH.   A reminder of our mortality; sometimes inter-
preted as the well-being of humans and animals. Ash is
the tree of rebirth.

BLACKBIRDS IN TREE.   Thoughts, imagination, and spirit
roosting in branches bare of foliage that await the
resplendence of spring.

BODY.   One's witness in the world, expressing their
highest hopes and deepest fears. Our bodies suffer
hurts and bear the marks of grief. Our bodies fail us,
and we despair. Yet the body is where we meet the soul
and experience joy, an expression of the divine. Our
bodies hold love and let it go; our voices say "love" and
then say something else. Delicate is the balance
between the external and internal worlds.

BONE.   Embodiment of life and resurrection.

BOW.   Signature of God's power. The arrow flying from
the bow represents the life force.

BUTTERFLY.   Symbol of the soul's rebirth and of attraction of the unconscious to light.

CAT.   Personification of the moon, and harbinger of
death.

CLOUDS.   Portents of metamorphosis.

CROWN.   An icon of the cosmic circle. The dropping of the crown made of antler and branches signifies the possibility of growth and regeneration.

DOLL.   A form representing the paralysis of creativity. The doll broken open reveals an emergence of creative forces.

 DRUM.   Instrument producing primordial sounds reminiscent of the heart. Also, earth's correlate for thunder and lightn.ng.

FABRIC.   A veil hiding truth or the deity. Also symbolic of the fragile boundary between spiritual and physical dimensions. The fabric in air, portraying fertility, suggests the possibility of creativity springing from divine union.

 FIRE.   Expression of spiritual energy signifying purification or passion.

FLUTE.   Instrument evoking the synthesis of male and female energies. Also associated with erotic or funereal events.

GRASSES/MEADOWS.   Landscape features associated with sorrow and infinite possibility.

 HAWK'S FEATHER.   Hawk personifies the soul's victory; its feather connotes emptiness, contemplation, and faith. The quill signifies the word.

NEST. A place of anticipation and nurture.

RING. A circle or musical arrangement expressing wholeness, wisdom, and light—nature's eternal song of creation and destruction.

ROCK/STONE. Epitome of solidity, permanence, and the dwelling place of God. Also suggestive of reconciliation with the self.

SHADOW. According to Jung, the instinctive side of the individual. Also, a vital part of wholeness.

SHELL. Manifestation of receiving and good fortune.

THORN. Of the wild thistle, associated with existence and nonexistence, pain and pleasure, ecstasy and anguish.

YEW. A reminder of nature's medicinal properties; also, a hard wood used to make archery bows. The tree of death.

ABOUT THE BOOK

This is a story of healing. It chronicles a series of encounters with the deepest part of myself following a letting go of all I had, for nothing else would release me from my body's excruciating pain. In giving expression to those encounters the pain was transformed into art.

The wounds I suffered were at the base of my spine, the result of surgery. The internal tissue, torn in three places, was not mending. Medication failed to provide relief, and additional surgery was not an option. Challenged every day by the simplest things, I hated what my body was doing to me and I wanted my old body back. The pain made me crazy: I stopped eating, closed my painting studio, and refused most company. I did not want to be who I had been, yet still I wanted my body back.

Desperate, I met with a body-centered healer who had years of experience in pain management. He told me that the only way he knew to relieve pain was by going deeper into it. My heart sank, because from my perspective I was in deep enough. Nevertheless, I agreed to open a door to the unknown and see what might happen.

After the first session, I experienced a movement of energy in my body. It was as if the pain had migrated further up my spine. "Had his hands done this?" I asked myself, mystified by the change.

Many sessions later, he taught me to meditate on the pain, to enter it and let it guide me. Meditation did not come easily since a mountain of mental constructs posed a huge impasse. Although obstructed and feeling controlled by thoughts, I somehow managed to inch toward the source of my struggle: the polarizing idea I had of wanting my body back and not wanting to be who I had been. With this discovery, meditation came more easily, and little by little the pain, my enemy, became my friend. Soon I saw it as a partner I could not imagine being without. At that point I gave up fighting who I was and in the process began to drop every little thing that had caused me pain.

One morning after meditating, I asked out loud, "God, give me a gift for the pain." It was not me speaking the words but rather the words speaking me. A reply echoed back from inside and outside of me: "Pick up a pen and write." I reached for a pen and proceeded to write, continuing the practice morning after morning until I had composed more than eighty poems. The next morning after meditation, an unfamiliar word escaped from my pen. This startling event led me deeper inside, where I opened an inner eye and saw how the external world informed my inner life, and vice versa. Continuing to write, I lost all awareness of the pain. By the time I had set down my pen, I was convinced that meditation was a powerful medication and the healing gift—language of the soul—had lifted me from body pain to body poetry.

After nearly a year of living with pain, my solitude had become solace. Now I could slip pain-free into the world of poetry, the bedchamber of an invisible lover made visible through words. Wind, water, buzzing bee …the sounds of nature escorted me daily to my soul.

About six months later I discovered external events affecting my internal life, a revelation that changed the poems radically. They began emerging from a place of greater knowing, recording experiences I sensed in my body. With or without pain, I wrote. I wrote because I loved it, because it saved my life, because it catalyzed my pain into a welcome creation. Then a palpable shift occurred: I could feel my body healing. Seeing parts of my body in nature and nature in my body, and realizing that they were one, I began documenting each inward visit in poems that now form the contents of this book.

When the poems were complete, I decided to illuminate the words with images. Accompanied by a photographer and three willing friends, I staged arrangements of my friends' bodies in nature—mostly in Washington's Methow Valley, a pristine corner of the world between Grizzly Mountain and Virginia Ridge. Next, I mounted copies of the photographs onto gessoed masonite and, using my fingers, enlivened each image with charcoal, acrylic paint, or other mediums, and occasionally collage, shedding light through the subject. I then framed each one, not to dress it up but to portray the image and its frame as one, scrubbing back the edges, light to dark, dark to light, to carry emphasis to the outermost bounds. On completion, over the surface of each piece I rubbed a cooled mixture of body ash and fire, sacred elements of remembrance and of transformation from one reality to another.

In the final stages of book design and layout, the creation pulsed on, now moved by a heartbeat of its own. A psalm began to form in short breaths on left-hand pages. Fragments would appear and disappear at odd intervals until the verse emerged in its entirety at the end. As it turned out, these exhalations, whispers from another layer of life, bore the promise of a burgeoning spring.

ABOUT THE AUTHOR-ARTIST

Margaret Jacoby Lopez, a visual artist and poet, was born and educated in Sydney, Australia. After graduating from the National Art School in Sydney, she continued her studies at the Academy of Art in San Francisco, where she received her master of fine arts degree. Since 1979, her paintings have appeared in more than twenty selected group exhibitions in Europe and the United States, and several solo exhibitions in California, Washington, and Oregon. Her work has also been auctioned for charities and is displayed in corporate collections nationwide. Publications containing her paintings, drawings, and poems range from sermons and books to the *Academy of Art Catalogue.*

Distinguished for her insights into color theory, Margaret provides individual training to artists, writers, and clergy exploring creativity as an avenue for spiritual growth. She currently resides in Santa Fe, New Mexico, where she is at work on a novel.